YOUR PRESENTATION IS A JOKE

BE LOVE
BE PEACE
BE FUNNY!

Marshall

Your Presentation is a Joke

EVERYTHING YOU NEED TO ABOUT ADDING HUMOR IN YOUR PRESENTATIONS TO MAXIMIZE YOUR IMPACT

Marshall Chiles

ISBN-13: 9781533175007
ISBN-10: 1533175004
Library of Congress Control Number: 2016901031
CreateSpace Independent Publishing Platform
North Charleston, South Carolina

DEDICATION

I dedicate this book to any presenter doing the work to go from good to great.

CONTENTS

ACKNOWLEDGMENTS

Thank you to all the great comedians I have worked with over the years who shared with me their writing techniques and process. Thank you to my Laughing Skull Lounge team of Ben Evans, Andrew George, and Bob Place.

A special thanks to my initial clients who took a chance and are now being rewarded with immortality in these acknowledgements: Paul Akers, Ben Kirshner and Scott Edinger. I also want to thank Greg Greenbaum for giving me the title of this book as the title was something I definitely struggled with. I mean, how do you title a book that is going to be more popular than the Beatles?

And of course I want to thank my family for being patient while I try to 'be more' in order to satisfy the five-year old little boy inside me.

INTRODUCTION

Who am I, why am I writing this book, and am I available for children's parties?

To start from the beginning... I was just seven years old when I knew I wanted to be a comedian. Like most comedians, I grew up poor, but my sisters and I didn't know we were poor because my mom lied to us about it. In fact, one Christmas she told my sisters that she had given them dolls, but they were really just empty bottles of Mrs. Butterworth's.

These days I am happily married with two kids. My friends ask me if we want to have a third kid, and I tell them that we are thinking about going back down to just one.

Please don't get me wrong, I like being a dad about 80 percent of the time. The other 20 percent of the time is when I have them.

I don't like using the words *my wife* because it sounds too possessive. So I just call Laura my ex-girlfriend.

Growing up, I had to contend with my share of bullies. It didn't take me long to realize that if I made someone laugh, they usually did not want to fight me. So you could say I became a funny guy in order to protect my pretty face.

As I look back now, I see I was using the comedy technique of distraction and replacing a negative branding image with a positive one.

I bet if those guys knew I was going to eventually refer to myself as a brand, they might have just gone ahead and hit me.

So, what qualifies me to write a book revealing how to inject humor into business presentations? What are my credentials?

For the past fifteen years, I've been doing stand-up comedy while building two successful comedy festivals and three comedy clubs. I've taught more than one hundred comedy classes, performed more than one thousand comedy shows, and produced more than five thousand comedy shows. I have built a comedy empire to pass off to my kids so they can eventually run it into the ground.

My presentation with the same name and content as this book won an award from the Young Presidents' Organization (YPO)—the world's largest network of chief executives under the age of forty. And I am the closing speaker for *Fortune* Magazine's Business Summit 2016.

I share these accomplishments not to make sure you know how wonderful I am, but to give you the confidence that your investment in this book is the best $59.95 you've ever spent. You did pay $59.95 didn't you?

Having said that, I've actually never really been comfortable calling myself a comedian because I have not had to make the sacrifice that "real comedians" have had to make.

I have friends who have lived in RVs, vans, and cars while struggling to make a living as aspiring comedians. I have other friends who were virtually homeless because they had to spend all their time on the road voyaging from black mold hotel to blood stained hotel for their gigs. They get to see the world and make drunken strangers accept them through laughter.

Although I have not stepped up and made this type of sacrifice, I feel I can make some claim to being a comedian because in my opinion a comedian is someone who can walk out onto a stage, stand there all alone in the glare of the hot spotlights, and tell their unique perspective to the world while staying truthful. And, of course, sometimes making people laugh.

I've been fortunate to have worked with some of the funniest people on earth: Robin Williams, Jim Gaffigan, David Chappelle, Jeff Foxworthy, and many, many more. I would keep name dropping, but name dropping isn't cool... Bob Saget taught me that.

I usually am a little intimated talking to these amazing human beings so I try to stay with a subject we both know, which is comedy. One of my favorite discussions with these great funny minds is the question: "How do you write?"

*Jim Gaffigan is awesome
and as nice as you imagine he is!*

Dave Chappelle is my favorite comedian.

Robin Williams is one of my heroes.

I've applied the lessons I have learned from these conversations—as well as from my own development as a comedian—into writing this book and my presentation. Today, I not only teach newbie comedians but I also add humor to numerous presentations for business presenters.

The ability to make a great presentation is an essential career builder. And a key element of any successful presentation is humor. Learning how to be funny isn't easy, but it is vital if you want to make an emotional connection with your audience that makes them like you.

I have developed several methodologies to help anyone be funnier when presenting. (Yes, even you!) This book teaches you how to use humor to make people take action or change their beliefs.

I appreciate that humor doesn't come naturally to most business presenters, least of all when you have a room full of potential clients staring at you and demanding to be informed while also being entertained.

Glossophobia is the fear of public speaking and Psychology Today published an article in 2012 stating that the fear of public speaking is greater than the fear of death. As Jerry Seinfeld observed, "This means to the average person, if you go to a funeral, you would rather be in the casket than doing the eulogy."

It doesn't have to be that way. That's why I've put together these methodologies that empower anyone to become funny. So if making presentations is essential to your career—carry on reading.

If you don't know how to present effectively, then you're going to bore your audience, lose business, get fired, or even worse. Death is always an option.

You don't want a bored audience.

*Your goals should be big enough to make
people question your judgment.*

The goal of this book is to untangle the web of humor and teach you how to use humor in your presentations in order to be more engaging and likable. Achieving these goals makes your presentation more effective in persuading people to take actions or change their beliefs. And—oh yeah—it will also make your business more successful… which is nice!

As I said (but it's worth repeating, trust me) I know all about "being funny" because I have been in the business of laughter for over fifteen-plus years. I've made it my livelihood as a comedy entrepreneur, and I can tell you it's not all that funny when people don't buy what you're selling. I have a business to run and need to generate revenue just like you. I feel your pain. So let me see if I can be your aspirin.

Here's how:

In this book I will explain the difference between comedy and humor. Most people have never thought about the difference, but there is a difference—just like motorcycles (comedy) are different from mopeds (humor).

I am a type A personality and have stripped down any fat I could find in delivering this information. In writing this book, I applied critical point analysis that states for any complex system there is a point where the smallest input produces the greatest output. Look at applying humor as the input that gives you the highest return for investindogs surfingg your resources (time/money). You can also look at this activity as Lean management as a form of kaizen; small, continuous improvements. AS you continuously make the small improvements, you will eventually see a huge improvement in your presentations.

However you look at it, my goal in this book to provide you with the highest rate of return for your investment of applying humor to your presentations to increase audience engaging and make you more likable. Remember, this book is dedicated to you. The few, the proud, the conference favorite.

The big take-aways for this book is:

1) You will learn the what & why of humor.
2) How to stay out of trouble with 'The Humor Rules.'
3) Comedy 101:The Fundamentals.
4) How to add funny images to your presentations.
5) You will learn how to write prepared humor so you can have your jokes in your pocket and let them come out organically.
6) How to write self-deprecating jokes.

I will provide you with a set of exercises so you can methodically add humor to your presentations. I will even show you how to "punch up a presentation" by including my audacious improvement of a great Steve Jobs speech.

As I said, the methodology that I teach in this book is a combination of all of my years conversing with and learning from people at the highest level of comedy artistry. I have taught these techniques to numerous executives and business presenters. So if you are asking yourself if you can really learn to be funny, let me show you this dog skateboarding:

*If this dog can learn to skateboard, which it
did, then you can learn to be funny.*

Being funny is no laughing matter. You have
to take it seriously. And it is hard work. If you're
ready... go ahead, roll up your sleeves, tap the
microphone—and let's get started.

Are you excited to get started?

CHAPTER 1

WHY HUMOR WORKS

Every communicator can use humor to communicate more effectively. Well, maybe not a drill sergeant. It's just not that intimidating to hear: "Drop and give me twenty giggles!"

If you're in a profession that requires you to communicate effectively with other people, and you are not in boot camp, you need to use humor.

Why humor? Because as Professor Jim Lyttle in 1977 explained after years of research, "humor increases persuasion's effectiveness." Stop and think about that. Humor increases persuasion's effectiveness. Makes sense, doesn't it? And one way humor increases persuasion's effectiveness is by distraction.

FACT: Every one of us has resistance to new people and new information. We can call this our "BS radar." When humor is used, it lowers our resistance and makes us more accepting of that new person and/or that information.

Over the years, some people have argued that the distraction humor causes is not such a good thing because it distracts from the message. I think those people are not only wrong but also boring. I'm sure you agree that nobody likes to listen to boring people.

But you don't just have to take my word for the value of humor in distraction. There's actual research to back it up. A study conducted at Amsterdam University titled "Those who laugh are defenseless: How humor breaks resistance to influence" looked into the "distraction" issue. What they found is that yes, indeed, humor distracts, and it is this distraction that lowers resistance. In a business setting, it replaces any negative brand association with more positive brand associations.

So, at the end of the day, humor works by distracting a person long enough to lower his resistance to the new information and then makes a positive association with the person/brand/computer screen that provided that humor to him.

The reality is that people want to be entertained more than they want to be educated. Brand owners have gotten wise to this and now connect with consumers by providing information in an entertaining manner. It's what the ad agency world has dubbed "infotainment." The new school of business teaches that if you do not deliver your information via infotainment, you lose out to those who do.

E-MOTION

Your message also needs to be emotionally compelling. What's the most important part of the word emotion? It's motion.

If you want to move people, then you need to connect to them emotionally. By providing the right kind of infotainment, you can connect to the audience and get them to move in your direction.

I submit that the best way to make that emotional connection is to use humor. Comedian Darryl Lenox says that it is essential for comedians to make that emotional connection in the first minute or else you will be fighting an uphill battle the rest of the show.

In order to better understand what emotions make people move, the *New York Times* hired two Penn State professors to study which emotion would most likely make content go viral. What they discovered was that at the top of the list for sharing content online was anger, followed by humor. So, unless you're some kind of angry dictator, humor is your best answer to connect with people.

Now before we go any further, let's consider the kind of business person you might want to be. You're almost certainly familiar with the terms B2B (Business to Business) and B2C (Business to Consumer).

IT IS *NOT* B2B OR B2C; IT IS H2H

I prefer to think of any business as being H2H. That stands for Human to Human. One of my favorite

3

sayings is: "It is not businesses doing business with other businesses—it is people doing business with other people."

All things being equal, you want to do business with your friends. All things being unequal, you still want to do business with your friends. If a potential client likes you, he is more likely to want to do business with you. Because—ultimately—the deciding person is just that, a person.

People want to feel good. They want to be happy. Scientific studies have shown that when a person smiles or laughs, his endorphins are raised, which makes him feel good. If you are the person who makes him feel that way, he will start to like you and become more likely to do business with you.

The *North American Journal of Psychology* reported in 2006 that "Making people smile or laugh increases your likability." No kidding. We need a scientific journal to tell us that? Yes, some of us do… but, since you are reading this book, I doubt you would argue against using humor.

Even the *Wall Street Journal* got in on the act, opining in a 2014 article: "Likability shapes how people are treated at work by bosses and co-workers."

For me, however, the most authoritative source is the late, great Johnny Carson who once said, "If people like you then you have won 80 percent of the battle."

Always be prepared for battle.

One good example of how this type of connection happened to me involved the annual event I run in Atlanta called The Laughing Skull Comedy Festival. That's when I bring together all kinds of great people connected with the comedy industry ranging from TV talent bookers, managers, agents, and Uber drivers.

A manager who has several celebrity clients called me a week after the most recent festival and told me that he wanted to find one project for us to work on together. He didn't know what. He just wanted to do business with me because he liked spending time with me whether in person or on the phone.

Result: we have already worked on two big projects—all stemming from the fact that we are kindred spirits who just wanted to work together. There was no big plan or specific earthshaking project. There was just an attitude of: "Let's figure out what we can do together." Again, people doing business with people.

In a way, it was like saying, "Let's play together," (because all work and no play makes divorce inevitable.)

Another story is from my good friend Mark Riccadonna who is a funny comedian and great actor. He once booked a dream job to film a commercial for a week on an island in the Caribbean. One night he went out drinking with the director and producer and asked them why they booked him for the gig. They said that he was not the best actor that auditioned, but he was good enough and Mark was someone they could see themselves spending a week with on an island.

Again, people want to do business with people they like.

LET'S PLAY

So, let's play. Now, you may or may not have heard about them, but there are studies that show that dogs will only play when they feel safe. They will *not* play if they feel threatened or if they are hungry. Subsequently, sociologists noticed the same is true for all animals, including humans. If you feel threatened or haven't had your Snickers, you will not be able to play.

When you use humor effectively, and someone smiles or laughs, that person is playing with you. That means you have made her feel safe. So, when you can use humor effectively, it makes an individual feel positive and it makes her feel safe, which then builds trust.

And once you have her trust, that is when you can get her money. After all, nobody will give you her money until you have gained her trust (or shown her some incriminating photos.)

Humor helps generate revenue.

7

On a side note, you won't laugh at someone if you don't trust him. That is why you should not try to use humor until you have established some trust or credibility.

The good news for business presenters is that you are usually seen as being credible simply because the event planner brought you in to speak to the group. Using humor is perfectly fine in this instance because of this preestablished credibility. It was done for you.

Use humor to build a stronger bond.

Now before we go further, it's important to understand the difference between *comedy* and *humor*. It is such an important topic that it needs a whole chapter to itself.

CHAPTER 2

THE DIFFERENCE BETWEEN COMEDY AND HUMOR

Comedy and humor. Aren't they one and the same thing? Absolutely not. The difference between comedy and humor is much like the difference between playing baseball and whiffle ball. They are both fun, but one is safer than the other and involves more alcohol.

Which leads us to the formula: comedy + business = humor

Humor is just safe comedy. Ultimately, humor is being funny while being non-offensive. The list of what offends people seems to be never ending. So the trick is to stay within what I call the "Humor Rules," which I discuss in more detail in the next chapter.

Comedy can go outside of social bounds and norms; humor does not have that luxury. Comedy can address race, sex, politics, and religion—pretty much anything, especially when it is within a comedy club setting. When you are in a business environment, however, these topics typically make people feel uncomfortable. They don't meet the rules of what's socially acceptable to discuss in public. (And if you don't know these social rules, and you are reading this book in public, please put your pants back on!)

Another big difference between comedy and humor is that comedy tends to be blunt and hard hitting while humor is more subtle and more cerebral. When you use humor, you are not trying to get the LOL ("Laugh Out Loud"), you are just trying to get the SOL ("Smile Or Laugh"). That is all you need in order to achieve increased engagement with your listener.

This book is not designed to make you LOL. My goal is to tickle your funny bone just enough to increase your engagement.

THE RIGHT TIMING

When is it appropriate to use humor in a presentation? Timing is everything of course, and not just in the delivery of a joke, but *when* you deliver it.

You've probably heard that an ideal time to use humor is at the beginning of a presentation. It's commonly said that "you always want to start off with a joke." And that's correct, because the faster you can make people laugh, the faster they will like you. Typically, you have eleven seconds to make a first impression. When people make a positive judgment of you within that short of a period of time, you're off to a flying start.

The other key time to add humor is during transition points. That's because, as author, professional speaker, and business trainer, Jeffrey Gitomer, once said, "People are paying the most attention just after you use humor because they want to hear what you are going to say next."

Humor makes them pay attention.

11

So employ humor during transition points, and it will train the audience to pay more attention.

Someone who appreciates the discipline of training more than most is famous Russian physiologist, Ivan Pavlov, who is best known for developing the concept of cognitive resonance when he trained a hungry dog to salivate at the sound of a bell. Pavlov conditioned the dog to associate the ringing of the bell with the sight of food. The same is true for when you use humor during your transitions. Your audience will become aware that there is a transition by the mere fact that you are using humor. Think of your audience as a pack of hungry, naked dogs, if you like.

Giving your audience cues is a successful technique used by several great comedians. Comedian George Burns's cue that he'd made a joke and it was time for the audience to laugh was when he paused and took a puff on his cigar.

Kathleen Madigan brings a drink on stage and when she wants the audience to laugh, she pauses and sips on her straw.

Rodney Dangerfield let the audience know it was time to laugh when he straightened his tie.

And my favorite comedian Dave Chappelle hits his leg with the microphone.

So to repeat: when you use humor during transition points, it keeps your audience engaged, and they get the subliminal message that you're transitioning, as well as understanding that it is their job to laugh.

Another important time to use humor is just before your key message. Remember what Jeffrey Gitomer said, the audience pays most attention just after humor. Now, if you can find a way to use humor in delivering your key message, it will have the most impact and will be remembered.

Research to validate that humor increases retention and recall comes from Dr. David Sousa, an international educational consultant and author of over twelve books on how the brain learns.

Dr. Sousa 2012 articles titled *Using Humor to Enhance Climate and Promote Retention* says that emotions enhance retention, so the positive feelings that result from laughter increase the probability that people will later recall the points you made.

So, if you have a key message in your presentation (and what kind of presentation doesn't?), the trick is to use humor just before—or during—that key message.

Laughs per Minute
Another difference between comedy and humor is laughs per minute (LPM).

When you are a comedian, your goal is to get as many LPMs as possible. The world record, by the way, is fifteen LPMs achieved by the great Phyllis Diller, who was a famous one-liner comedienne in the 1950s. She clocked at one LOL every four seconds…bam, bam, bam, and BAM!

What I don't like about office Christmas parties is having to look for a job the next day.
—Phyllis Diller

Now, when using humor in a presentation, it's an entirely different matter. You only want to be funny every three to five *minutes*, because if you do it more than that, it becomes too distracting. It becomes more of a comedy routine than a business presentation. Everything has a bell curve for maximum effectiveness, including humor in your presentations.

There is a very famous saying...

Dying is easy; comedy is hard.

It's true—comedy is very hard. It takes most people years to become proficient at comedy. After all, its just you, alone on that stage or standing at that podium, with a microphone and an audience, going through your therapy called comedy.

But there is some good news—although comedy is hard, *humor* is easy. Especially in a business climate.

The reason why humor is easy is because the corporate bar has been set so low that all you have to do is make a valiant effort, and you win!

There is a low bar for funny in business presentations.

Oh, yes. This is what happens when the bar is set too low! And I'm making another point here about utilizing illustrations in a presentation (more on that later.)

I'm sure, like me, you have sat through your share of boring presentations. Actually, if you're like me, you probably find *most* people's presentations are not very engaging, but they do give you time to mentally prepare your to-do list for the following day.

When you see somebody make a determined effort to be humorous you think, "Oh, thank goodness!" Because either they will be intentionally entertaining, or maybe not so intentionally entertaining.

Repeat: while comedy is hard, humor is easy. All you have to do is make a valiant effort, and you win!

As I mentioned earlier, though, there are some rules that have to be obeyed. Otherwise, you're courting disaster. We'll explore those next.

CHAPTER 3

The Humor Rules

I n comedy, the rules are vague. In humor, the rules are etched in stone—and that stone is made out of years of lawsuits wrapped in severance packages!

Remember…

COMEDY + BUSINESS = HUMOR

This equation means that if you want to use comedy in a business setting, you need to follow the rules for humor. There is a reason that Humor Rules has the same initials as Human Resources. So make sure you write jokes that are HR approved.

Many newbie stand-up comedians hired for corporate gigs have been perplexed when the joke that kills at the comedy club gets zero laughs at a company event. They just weren't mindful of the fact that humor for a business audience is different from comedy for club appearances.

Some reasons for the rejections of the jokes are obvious, while others are not so obvious. After years of writing jokes for corporate clients, I have found the following "rules" apply to any kind of presentation in a business setting:

1) **Keep it above the belt.**

   Do not make any reference to sex, sexual relations, or private body parts. You may think it is cute, but others may think it is inappropriate or possibly even creepy, and it makes them uncomfortable. No sexual innuendos. You don't want your audience squirming in their seats. So keep it above the belt, but below the chest, and then pick it up again around the knees. You don't want to rub anyone the wrong way... pun intended.

2) **Stay away from religion and politics.**

People are very passionate about their religion and politics (even though everyone has it wrong except for you and your Facebook friends). In the workplace, you don't want to make "jokes" about these two subjects because someone is more than likely going to disagree with you and be offended. Not everyone is as well informed and logical as you are!

And even outside the workplace, these subjects can be tricky. If you meet someone at a party, for example, and he immediately starts flexing his religious or political beliefs, you might be taken aback. Even if you agreed with the "maniac," you would probably not want to spend too much time with him and would escape as quickly as possible to hang out with the guacamole dip.

3) **Do not make fun of any one person or group of people.**

This means no joking about genders, nationalities, and so forth… unless you look around and don't see any of them near you.

When you want mass appeal, you cannot, for example, make fun of German people. Sure, they may be an "acceptable" target, but they have taken on the world twice and almost won. Don't make them angry.

4) **Stay away from words with violent images.**

The idea of using humor is to make people feel upbeat and *positive.* When you use a word that has a violent connotation, you are putting disturbing imagery in their heads, and most definitely not making them feel positive. Such a word, as an example, is *Holocaust.* The diabolical images associated with this word—no matter how you use it—will slow down and distract your listener, and could actually upset some people.

Using words of this nature are a major distraction and will trigger thoughts in the minds of your audience that will take them way off topic and give you negative brand association.

5) **Stay away from references to drugs.**

You may think getting three DUIs is funny, but I assure you that the human resource director and legal department do not.

You may even party with your CEO, but dare to crack (pun intended) one joke about cocaine, and you become a pariah.

6) **Stay away from unsafe subjects.**

What's an unsafe subject? Let's say you're the CEO, and you make some kind of joke about laying off people. Not funny under any circumstance. Unless, of course, you are a short-term shareholder and get to laugh all the way to the bank.

Follow these six rules, and they will keep you out of trouble with 99 percent of the people you work with. For the other 1 percent, you probably didn't want to work with that person anyway.

Do I think that having to abide by these rules makes you less funny? Nope! On the contrary, there is a popular opinion in the art community that "constraint enhances creativity."

When someone is given a limited box to work in, he has a focal point that generally makes him more creative. A 2014 Fast Company article titled *Proof that Constraints Can Actually Make You More Creative* points out that having constraints actually helps you get over writer's block. The idea of creating with no restraints means you have insurmountable options to choose from. Restrictions take away some of your choices and therefore reduces the paralysis of choice that keeps people from getting started.

So, you can look at these Humor Rules as a liability or an asset. I suggest the positive perspective, and so does your high school counselor.

Being in a box is fun!

INTERNAL HUMOR VERSUS EXTERNAL HUMOR

The most important place to obey these six humor rules is during external communication. You know your own company's culture, and it might be "cool" with cursing or slightly off-color jokes. But you do not know other companies' cultures. Try telling a race-based joke in a pitch meeting with Coca-Cola, and then see how fast it takes you to collect unemployment.

So be smart about using humor with people outside of your company. Until you know them well enough to break the humor rules, obey the humor rules.

Learn the rules like a pro, so you can break them like an artist.
—Pablo Picasso

Yes, I know you didn't expect to be reading about rules in a comedy book. Rules are never funny, are they? But they're necessary—as are some other fundamentals that we need to cover before you can become the funniest you can be.

CHAPTER 4

COMEDY FUNDAMENTALS

The secret to comedy is surprise.
—ARISTOTLE 470 BC

The secret to surprise is misdirection.
—MARSHALL CHILES 2016 AD

The element of surprise is key.

Have you ever had someone tell you a joke you've heard before? Undoubtedly, that's happened. And you probably didn't laugh because you knew the ending (unless you were being extremely polite, sympathetic, or you were trying to sell the person something). But when the surprise was gone, so was the funny. It's the same when someone tells you a joke and you see the punch line coming a mile away. You don't laugh; you are like: "Yeah, whatever dude. Just make it large fries."

MISDIRECTION

So, you have to keep the ending a surprise. One of the best methods to create surprise is what's called "misdirection." Misdirection is huge in comedy. In fact, it's huge in the world in general. I mean, if you get people distracted, you can do whatever you want.

If you were paying attention (and not distracted) you'll remember I discussed in the introduction how I distracted kids from beating me up by becoming the funny guy. It was distraction that had these guys go from wanting to punch me in the face to walking away laughing… while I went home to do more push-ups.

Misdirection is a major tool of the trade for magicians, too. Magicians make you pay attention to what's happening in their right hand while manipulating the situation with their left hand (while still disappointing their parents.)

Magic is based on misdirection... of a career.

How do you create misdirection?

The easiest form of misdirection is the "rule of three." And the easiest rule of three for business presenters is:

Serious
Serious
Funny

The first two items are legit, and the third item is a surprise. You get to make your point with the first two items, and then you get to entertain with the third item.

Misdirection works by making people think you are taking them down an obvious path, but then you take them in an alternate direction. Notice in the accompanying illustration that the path on the right looks like the obvious trail. It looks like you are going to follow that path. But, in reality, you will make a quick turn and head on down the path on the left. It's the same with comedy.

But in order for the punch line to work, the starting point has to make sense. The best way to understand this is to give you an example.

Here goes: "Giving 110 percent takes hard work, dedication, *and a complete disregard for how math works.*"

That works. That's an obvious connection between the beginning projected path and the surprise path.

But now let's try this: "Giving 110 percent takes hard work, dedication, and knowing how to salmon fish." What?

See the difference? One hundred and ten percent is related to math. Therefore, both the beginning and ending correspond. However, salmon fishing has nothing to do with the beginning part of the trail, that is, math. Not funny. If you are going to use misdirection, the punch line—the surprise at the end—has to correspond with the beginning.

QUANTITY = QUALITY

In being creative, you can only get quality by doing quantity. This is the hard and fast rule of "practice makes perfect." When you first start juggling, for example, you are going to drop some pins. But eventually, after much practice, you will get good enough at juggling so that you only end up dropping your friends.

When Drew Carey was starting out as a comedian, he had a rule that he would write ten jokes a day, every day. At the end of the week (if my math is any good) he had seventy jokes. If only two or three of them were acceptable, after a year, he had about 100–150 new jokes. That's a 4 percent success rate. How about that? To produce a 4 percent success rate, you better be producing some quantity. And the good news: you don't need to be as funny as Drew Carey.

Drew Carey's goals for being funny are probably loftier than yours. When presenting in business, you don't need a belly laugh. Remember, for business presentations, you only need to get the smile or slight laugh to win. (Much like what I am doing in this book).

However, although you may not be trying to be as funny as Drew Carey, his work ethic illustrates the level of effort needed to find the "real funny."

Don't set a low bar. Look at the time spent on your writing/creating like going to the gym. If you try to compete on a level akin to players in the NBA (assuming you're eight feet tall), you need to go to the gym more often than 99.99 percent of other people. But if you compete against people who don't even go to the gym, you are more likely to win with just a few practices.

As a creative writer, your gym is a yellow note pad and pencil. (OK, MS Word can work, too). If you want to be head and shoulders above others in your field, you need more time in the gym. So for you, doing the work of "quantity = quality" means that the longer you practice the humor, the better you will become… so congratulations, you are the least funny you will ever be!

Jerry Seinfeld still writes every day and has come up with a system to help keep him on track. On his calendar he marks a red *X* for every day that he writes jokes. I submit that if presenting is a key part of your work life, then you should do the same—except your *X* represents the time you spend on your presentation. Your goal should be to get as many *X*'s in a row as possible and to never break that chain.

Again, you're not trying to be the next Jerry Seinfeld (or are you?). But if you want to excel at humor, and presenting, you need to practice: "quantity = quality."

Another major benefit from writing in quantity is that it helps drive you to get past what we in the comedy world call the "go-to joke." The go-to joke is the low hanging fruit that is easy to see. If it is too easy to see, it is not a surprise. If it is not a surprise, it is probably not as funny. So keep working at it.

You can't achieve a million-dollar dream
with a minimum-wage work effort.
—Author Unknown

Quantity raises the quality bar.

Let me provide another example of the benefits of quantity. It comes from the book *Art and Fear* by David Bayles and Ted Orland. They share a story where a professor gave two sets of students the task of making the perfect cooking pot within a thirty-day period.

The first group was instructed to spend all of their time making just one pot. The second group was told to make as many cooking pots as they could. So their focus was on quantity.

Guess what? At the end of the thirty days, the students in the quantity group made a better pot than the students who focused single-mindedly on just one pot. Why did the quantity group have a better pot? Because they were able to learn from their mistakes and kept making better and better pots.

This story reminds me of the saying: "Ready, shoot, aim."

Repeat: "Quantity = Quality."

Don't Edit What Is Coming Out of You; Edit Once It Is Already Out of You

So many people second guess themselves when they write. But the best way to write is to focus on the writing, not the editing.

The first step to writing is to get all your thoughts "on paper" and then edit what is there.

When you squeeze an orange, you get orange juice. When you squeeze a lemon, you get lemon juice. So when you write, squeeze what is inside of you, and let that come out naturally.

When you are thinking of funny words, or writing anything, remember:

Don't edit what is coming out of you; edit once it is already out of you.

Again, like with most activities, the more you create humor, the easier it will be. Eventually, you will deliver faster and better jokes not just in writing, but in conversation, too. One of my first clients, Paul Akers, told me that his wife of 30 years now finds him funny thanks to our work together on his TEDx talk.

BREVITY

Brevity is the soul of wit.
—William Shakespeare

Truly, I find this quote ironic because William Shakespeare's name is almost as long as his quote. So if Shakespeare really believed in brevity, why didn't he go by Billy Shakes? (Yeah, nobody laughs at this joke in real life, either.)

Cut to the chase.

The shorter the time to the funny ending, the better. If the wording is too lengthy, people's minds can wander… and their faces usually wander to their cell phones.

The way to brevity is simple:

1) If you can turn two words into one, do it.
2) If you can turn two sentences into one, do it.

Here's an example:

Version one: GOOD
"I like being a dad about 80 percent of the time. The other 20 percent of the time, I have them."

versus

Version two: BAD
"I am a father of two boys, five and eight years old. They are named Harper and Nolan. I do like 80 percent of the things about being a dad. Then with the rest of the time, I have them."

Version one: twenty-one words
Version two: forty words

Those extraneous words have a negative impact on the joke. The more superfluous words you use, the more wasted time, the more mind wondering, and less impact.

French mathematician and philosopher Blaise Pascal famously wrote to someone: "I'm sorry I wrote you such a long letter; I didn't have *time* to write a short one." Over the years, Pascal's quote has been shortened (brevitied) to say, "If I had more time, I would have written less." So even one of the original masters of brevity, could still do some more brevity. I bet all your presentations can be more brevitied. (it's a word now)

I bet you didn't expect to be reading a quote from a French mathematician and philosopher in a book on humor, did you? I also bet you also probably didn't expect to read about fairy tales. Read on!

BREAD CRUMBS

When focusing on brevity, you are really looking at the words you have chosen for your talking points. I like to look at my words as bread crumbs. Do you remember the story of Hansel and Gretel? How the siblings walked in the forest dropping bread crumbs behind them so they could find their way back home? Not a bad idea until the birds came along and ate their bread crumbs. Leaving Hansel and Gretel to a life threatening challenge. And don't you feel like you want to die when your joke doesn't work? That feeling should inspire you to focus on the right words when creating the funny.

When looking at your words as bread crumbs, you want to use the least amount of bread crumbs as possible. Do you need all of your bread crumbs on the trail? Or are you just feeding the birds and putting your life in danger?

The bread crumbs lead to the bread loaf, not vice versa. Another good way to brevity is to think of each word costing you one hundred dollars. Now you will start to find whatever way you can to lower the number of words used.

In the previous joke example, about being a dad, there was no need for me to tell you how old my sons are or their names. That was unnecessary information. The only reason to have included those details would be if they were relevant to the punch line.

Therefore, if you have bread crumbs that have nothing to do with the surprise ending, get rid of them, because they are for the birds.

Too many bread crumbs can make your audience go crazy.

On the other hand, make sure that all of the vital bread crumbs are kept in place. Have you ever had a joke fall flat and then have to say…"Oh. I forgot to tell you the guy was a doctor."

Being a doctor was an important bread crumb leading the way to the punch line.

PUT PUNCH WORD AT THE END

Let me emphasize again, the whole concept of funny is… surprise. Which is why you want to put your punch word at the very end of your joke, or as close to the end as possible.

Here's an example from a CEO client who attends big sales presentations and introduces the presenting sales rep with:

> BAD
> "I'm only here to pick up the check. I'm not going to be adding any value to the presentation."

It would have been so much better if he'd said:

> GOOD
> "I'm not going to be adding any value to the presentation. I'm only here to pick up the check."

And with an emphasis on the word *check*. The last word is where the funny is.

Comedy great, and legend, Mitch Hedberg.
Please Check him out on YouTube.

Or as one-liner comedian Mitch Hedberg says, "This shirt is dry clean only. Which means (pause) it's dirty."

And with an emphasis on the last word.

(Note the *pause* as we will be discussing these further in the chapter about delivery.)

Putting the punch word anywhere else is like eating dessert before your appetizer. If you do that, then you are probably two years old—and what are you doing reading this book?

When you put the punch word at the end, *that* is where the surprise is—and is supposed to be. If you talk past the punch word or punch line, you are doing what comedians sometimes call "going past the post office." You delivered the goods and kept on going.

When you keep going past the funny, you do the listener a grave disservice. You don't give them the opportunity to laugh.

Here's another example using one of the jokes with which I opened this book:

GOOD
"I grew up poor, but we didn't know we were poor because my mom was always lying to us about it. I remember one Christmas. She gave my sisters dolls, but they were really just empty bottles of Mrs. Butterworth's."

Note that the punch word is "Mrs. Butterworth's." I placed that phrase at the very end because that is the surprise ending. It would not be much of a surprise if it were in the beginning like this:

BAD
"My mom used to give my sisters empty bottles of Mrs. Butterworth's for Christmas, because we were poor, and she told them it was a doll."

Do you see how word placement is so crucial? If you put the surprise word anywhere other than at the end, you're diminishing the surprise and effectiveness.

Great comedians get to the punch line as quickly as possible. One of the lines I like to use (and you can use a variation for no extra charge) is: "I am married with two kids. Which means I am very happy to be here."

So speed is important, as is sound. Here's what I mean.

USE WORDS WITH HARD CONSONANTS

Hard consonant words stick in the ear better and make more of an impact. Words that have the letter P, D, K, or T usually do the trick.

Examples: carrot, pants, car, locker, potato, and almost every word of profanity, but we'll cover that later.

Would you agree that pants sounds funnier than jeans?

Carrot pants just sounds funny.

In one episode of the TV show *The Simpsons*, the character Krusty the Klown had a scarf wrapped around his neck. Someone asked what was wrong with him, and Lisa Simpson said that he had hurt his throat using a punch line containing too many hard consonants. Considering that *The Simpsons* has won thirty-two Emmys, I think we can all agree that the show's writers know a trick or two about writing funny.

Another great example of the power of hard consonants comes from the highly successful Sara Blakely. Sara started and built a company called Spanx. Before she started her amazing business journey, she was in the Atlanta comedy scene for a hot minute. She learned that words with the K sound stick in the ear best. So when coming up with her company name, she wanted a K sound in it.

Look at the word Spanx... one syllable with two hard consonant sounds and a one billion dollar valuation.

By now you're hopefully beginning to understand that comedy isn't something that just happens out of the clear blue sky. Even people who were supposedly "born funny" have to work at it. There are proven practices that you can learn that can make you funnier. And, if you haven't guessed, I'm setting you up for the next chapter, which introduces my three-step process to make you funnier.

On a related note about art and methodology, many lead singers in bands first hum a song before finding the words to match that humming pattern. Yes, even something as "artistic" as a lead singer in a band has a methodology to help find her words.

Even rock stars have a method.

So with that, let me show you what methodology you can employ to be funnier.

CHAPTER 5

ADDING FUNNY IMAGES

One of the easiest and fastest ways to get a laugh in a presentation is with visual images.

In fact, with the right picture you can convey in literally an instant what might take thirty seconds of words to explain.

And yes, I have a methodology for this solution as well. Here's how:

Step One: Do a search on Google Images. Enter the word *funny* and the "subject" of your key message. Search variations of your key word using Thesaurus.com. (I know you know about this website, but do you use it yet?)

Step Two: When you find the picture that you want to use to enhance your presentation, copy the image URL and then go the website www.TinEye.com. When put the image URL in TinEye.com you can find the original source and the biggest file for that image. Sometimes you will find an image but it has been turned into a meme and has words on it which makes using it impossible. When you go to TinEye.com and find the original source, it usually is meme-free and has no words on it so then you can use that image.

> **Important:** Don't use professional photos such as Getty Images or iPhoto unless you plan to pay for them. These companies have bots searching the web for images they own and making sure the user has permission for that image. They will then send you a notice saying you owe them $800 (or whatever) for using their image without permission. So if you find an image you really want to use and it is a professional image, you should go ahead and buy it with the appropriate usage fee.

> I purposely look for unprofessional pictures because I think they are funnier. I have found many funny photos on eastern European blogs.

Step Three: Then your mission is to write a funny line incorporating your message that complements the picture.

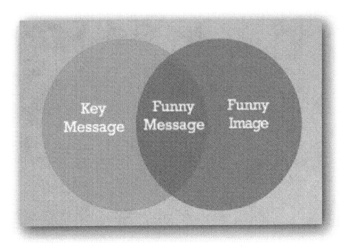

Yes, I will give you some examples on the following pages.

EXAMPLE ONE
Your message concerns customer service.

Subject: Customer Service

Google Images search:

> Funny customer service
> Funny service
> Funny phone handling
> Funny phone

Here's the image you might find:

Not everyone takes customer service seriously.

The image and the matching message get a chuckle every time!

EXAMPLE TWO
Your message concerns providing solutions.

Subject: Providing Solutions

Google Images search:

> Funny providing solutions
> Funny solutions
> Funny answers
> Funny searching

Eventually, you will find an image like this:

Some people have no idea where to find solutions.

EXAMPLE THREE
Your message is in regard to finding customers.

Subject: Finding Customers

Google Images search:

    Funny finding customers
    Funny customers
    Funny demographic
    Funny audience

Here's an image that might turn up:

We know how to reach your audience.

And one more…

EXAMPLE FOUR
Key message is solutions.

Google Images search:

    Funny solutions
    Funny answers
    Funny options
    Funny choices

Here's a good image:

People can find their options confusing.

This image gets a laugh as soon as people see the sign because they can relate to it.

Images create an entirely different dimension to presentations and can make your points much more memorable. Use them to hit home with many messages.

If you are going to go down this road of using funny images, I **highly suggest** you make a folder to file <u>all</u> of the funny photos you find. Even if you do not have a specific need for a funny photo you find, go ahead and put it in your 'Funny Photos' folder because you might fins a use for it later. Using a 'Funny Photos' folder will be a timesaver for future presentations.

Another way to effectively insert humor is with just words and we will learn the process for that in the next chapter.

CHAPTER 6

THE THREE-STEP PROCESS

A ll comedians have a process. And, at some point, they ditch it to follow their gut.

Your stomach knows more than your brain does.

If you are experienced enough to not need a process, then you are probably not reading this book. And since you are reading this book, you do need a process.

After spending many years writing comedy and talking to great comedians about comedy writing, I've put together a simple, three-step methodology along with a series of exercises that will help make you funny.

Note, I wrote *simple* and not *easy*. The reason you may find these exercises challenging is because it is new to you. And when you start something new, it is usually difficult. The more you do it, however, the better you get at it.

With the following three steps, you will begin to see the same subject from many different angles. But all these angles have one thing in common, and that is the "truth." I'm sure you have heard the phrase that "it's funny because it's true." Well, that is… true.

Now it's time for you to do some work. Are you ready? Don't give up now.

Step One: Statements of Truth
This is the most important step, because we want to be truthful and authentic when we present and when we are being funny.

There are blank exercise forms at the back of this book, and you can download copies of all these exercises at www.HumorWins.com/resources.

Choose a subject, and then write all the statements you can think of that are true about that subject.

STATEMENTS OF TRUTH

Subject: _____

_____

_____

_____

_____

_____

_____

_____

_____

_____

_____

_____

Again, this step is very important because this is where you will write *your* truth. Does it apply to 100 percent of other people? Probably not.

I believe that everyone's reality is as unique to them as their thumbprints. But our realities also have lots of Venn diagram overlays.

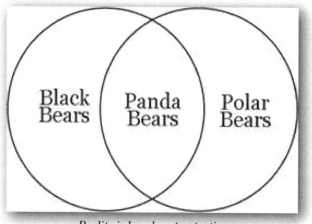

Reality is based on perspective.

Next, write how you feel about the subject. And do *not* overthink this. If I were doing this exercise with you at a seminar, I would ask you to fill in the blank: "The way you feel about (subject) is ___." And I'd make you answer right away, so you wouldn't agonize and think too long about it. Remember, we don't edit what is coming out, we edit once it is out.

How many truths are there? The answer is three—yours, mine, and the video. But you want to write as many "statements of truth" as possible. The more the better... and it helps you dig a little deeper into truth.

Step Two: Lists
Look at the next exercise titled "Lists." This step is where you write all of the words you can think of that are associated with your subject (nouns, verbs, adjectives, etc.).

Keep digging until you make your point.

This list exercise is an excellent way to start finding the different angles to a subject. When you come across an even more difficult subject, you can take extra time and actually make three lists: one each for nouns, verbs, and adjectives.

When you get this detailed, you should be able to compile a comprehensive list of words from which you can select the connections for a surprise ending.

The best tool for digging up a selection of word options is: www.Thesaurus.com.

LISTS

Subject: _____

_____	_____	_____
_____	_____	_____
_____	_____	_____
_____	_____	_____
_____	_____	_____
_____	_____	_____
_____	_____	_____
_____	_____	_____

Step Three: * I emotion subject because

Now, this is where you can really start to look at the subject differently. You use emotions like: love, hate, fear, excitement, worry, and so forth.

I hate SUBJECT because ___ , I love SUBJECT because ___

You then complete the sentence trying to use words from step two and your "statements of truth" from step one. In this step, as in all the steps, stay as honest as possible when generating your ideas.

Start with the emotion of "hate" and then move to "love." These are the strongest emotions, and if you end with the angle of "love," you'll discover that your surprise ending has a more positive tone (as well as being more acceptable).

* saracsm

Yes, you can use other emotions when digging deep into a subject, but starting off with these two is easiest and best, because they are the strongest emotions.

If these two emotions do not find the right "funny" for you, and you feel you are onto something, feel free to pick a few other emotions to try. It's your call.

Fill in the blanks and use various emotions. The more emotions you use on the subject, the more angles you will find. And you also add the word *because__* to help you justify your emotions.

However, if you can use other words to relate to that subject, that's good, too. For example, *but* (He-he, I said *but*.) can also create some various fun endings (surprises).

* center?

"I (emotion) (subject) because: _____"

_____

_____

_____

_____

_____

_____

_____

CHAPTER 7

EXAMPLE OF THE THREE-STEP PROCESS

O K, numerous studies show that the best way to learn is by example. So, I will show you an example by performing the three-step process using the subject of "traffic."

The first step is:

STATEMENTS OF TRUTH

Subject: Traffic
Traffic makes me frustrated.
Traffic can sometimes make me angry.
There are lots of cars with only a single person in them.
Traffic reports never mention the road I am on when I am on it.
Traffic makes me feel competitive.
Traffic is worse when it is in gridlock.

Are these statements the same as what you would say? Probably—at least a few of them. So, these are truths that others may see as well.

Step two is to make the list of words associated with your subject.

LISTS

Subject: Traffic

cars	buses	on the phone
frustrated	accidents	texting
bored	competitive	facebook
traffic reports	commute	late
judgmental	gridlock	carbon dioxide
pollution	buses	stalled car

Note that I am using some of the same words I used in the statements of truth. The list here is short, but it gives you an idea of how you put words down from the statements of truth and from other sources. Remember, www.Thesaurus.com is a great tool for coming up with words for this "list" exercise.

And when selecting what words to finish the sentence remember to use words with hard consonants.

Now, let's find the hard consonant words to finish the sentences in the next step, which is:

"I (emotion) (subject) because: _____ "
I hate traffic because:

> It makes me frustrated.
> People changing lanes makes me feel competitive.
> Traffic reports never mention the road I am on when I am on it.
> I don't like looking at other people in gridlock.
> It makes me more judgmental.
> It encourages me to bike to work.
> It puts out so much carbon dioxide.

Then reverse the feeling of "hate" in order to deliver the surprise. Thus, you take the "hate" sentence and turn it into why you "love" it. That makes it funny. Along with *the way* you say it, of course. (Delivery will be covered in a later chapter.)

"I (emotion) (subject) because: _____ "
I love traffic because:

> I like starting my day frustrated.
> It really brings out my competitive side.

I get to hear about the traffic on other people's commutes.

I like the sense of community you can only find in gridlock.

It reminds me of how judgmental I am.

It reminds me that I made the right decision to bike to work.

I like to start my day off with the sweet smell of carbon dioxide.

This exercise helps you uncover different ways to address a subject, but it might not be a finished product of: "I love (subject) because ___." What the process does do, though, is allows you to approach a subject from different angles and use key words and key emotions/perspectives to find the "funny."

Here are the jokes on traffic that come from this exercise:

"I hate traffic because I do not like the smell of carbon dioxide" is now "I love traffic because I like to start my day with the sweet smell of carbon dioxide."

Remember the goal is to eventually be able to find and write the "funny" from your "gut." So, listen to your gut. Write lots of jokes. Then, use the one that gets you the most excited.

Tell the jokes that get you most excited.

CHAPTER 8

MISDIRECTION EXERCISE

Will my three-step methodology work 100 percent of the time? No. It will not. The only thing that works 100 percent of the time is Murphy's law.

So, here is one more exercise that can help you find the funny/surprise in (almost) any subject.

MISDIRECTION

Write the sentence:

_____
_____
_____

Verbs/nouns/adjectives/prepositions:

_____
_____
_____

Opposite and associated verbs, nouns, adjectives, prepositions, etc.:

_____

_____

_____

Look at the blank example of the misdirection exercise.

1) Write the sentence at the top of the sheet of paper.
2) Find the key words, which are the verbs, nouns, and adjectives.
3) Find the opposite and associated words of those key words. (Remember the magic that is Thesaurus.com.)

The next step is to mix the sentence up using one or two of the opposite words in place of the key words.

Write the sentences mixing the opposite verbs/nouns/adjectives/prepositions, one to two at a time:

_____

_____

_____

As you start to write these sentences, you can find some fun surprise endings.

When writing these mixed sentences, please be open to many possibilities. What at first you think is crazy (or too dirty) could be the stepping stone to the surprise that makes sense *or* that you help make sense.

Here is a sample of performing my misdirection exercise:

MISDIRECTION

Write the sentence:
The journey of a thousand miles begins with the first step.

Verbs/nouns/adjectives/prepositions:
Journey, one thousand, miles, begins, first step

Opposite and associated verbs, nouns, adjectives, prepositions, etc.:
Sitting, waiting, one, infinity, inches, kilometers, end, last, jump, sit, stand, skip

Note that since this is a short sentence, there is little difference in the number of words between the sentence and the key words. Additionally, note that there is more than one opposite word for some of the words in the original sentence.

Now, we start mixing words to form various sentences until we find what works for us. The finished product can look very different every time. That is normal, so please, keep calm and write on.

Stay relaxed, and it all works out.

Remember, the goal of all comedy writing exercises is to get you to look at the original sentence from different angles. So here is what I came up with:

MISDIRECTION

A journey of one thousand miles begins with the first step:

> But sitting for one day can be the best reward.
> But sitting for one thousand hours begins with someone calling "shot gun."

And waiting for one thousand hours begins
with walking into the DMV.
And ends with one thousand hours of sitting.
And ends with a new pair of shoes.
(Bingo, we have a winner.)

Are any of these LOL? No, not in my opinion. But remember that we are not going for LOLs, we are going for SOLs. I submit that a couple of these jokes might be good enough for corporate humor, if delivered correctly.

The line I would choose is "...and ends with a new pair of shoes."

Another way you can use misdirection is to write out what you think the next logical sentence would be. And then you just reverse it. Start writing sentences that are the opposite of the next logical sentence.

Here is a great misdirection joke by comedian Sarah Silverman:

"When I was in high school, I went out with my father's best friend. And that's embarrassing, you know, my father having a 14-year-old best friend."

The first part makes you think that she is dating someone her dad's age. Then she changes the anchor age to her, not her father. The punch line works because she surprised you and made her dad's friend her age.

Remember, the way misdirection works is that you make the audience think you are going one direction, and then—boom!—you take the opposite direction by making a hard left or right, or you turn yourself around. In any case, please don't do the hokey-pokey.

OK. Are you getting the hang of it? If so, it's time to show you how to enhance any presentation.

Remember, the projected ending and surprise ending have the same beginning.

69

CHAPTER 9

PRESENTATION PUNCH-UP

Just about any presentation can be finessed and improved. It's a simple process (yes, another process!) that I call "presentation punch-up." Doing this exercise allows you to hit it and forget it.

The very funny comedian Christopher Titus is known for being a master story teller who can take the most delicate subject and make it funny. He taught me this five-step formula years ago and I can tell you that it definitely works.

NOTE: Titus taught me this exercise for adding the funny to stories. I am changing the word 'story' with the word 'presentation' because that is why you are reading this book.

It's only five steps, and no, it's not a dance. (What do I have against dancing? Nothing. Let's do this!)

Step One: Write your presentation without trying to add any humor.

Step Two: Take the first sentence you want to make funny and put it on a separate sheet of paper.

Step Three: Now, look at that sentence and write as many jokes/humor points as possible for that one sentence.

Step Four: Then, put that sentence back into the presentation with your joke of choice. How do you pick which joke? It's the one you are most excited to tell.

Step Five: Go to the next sentence you want to make funny and re-do steps two through four.

Pretty simple, right?

I bet you are confused as I am about how to do step number three.

Put the subject through that three-step process, and you should be able to find some funny for your chosen sentence.

And, remember: quantity = quality. In order to be effective at discovering the "funny," you need to practice just like you'd practice football, tennis, or toe wrestling. (Yes, that is a real sport.)

Is the time you spend punching up your presentation going to earn you more money? Well, I think you would say yes to that question or else you would not be reading this book!

Are you willing to do the work?

I once heard that only 5 percent of people will actually do the work required to use new information.

Think about it. If that statistic is true, it means even though one hundred people might agree that it is worth the investment of time to do the work to be more effective at presenting, only five will actually do it. Are you in that five percent? Or are you going to sit down and watch more reality TV this evening?

Are you willing to do the work? After all, *comedy writing exercise* has the word *exercise* in it because that's what it is. If it were easy, it would be called "comedy writing naps."

I once saw a VHS tape of comedy legend Larry Miller tell a group of college students that in order to be on the level of someone like Michael Jordan, you need to do the work like Michael Jordan. So, when it comes to developing your humor/presentation/sales pitch/and so forth, are you going to the gym *every* day? Are you running stadiums at five in the morning? Are you writing at five in the morning? How about being the first one on the court/computer and the last one off the court/computer? If you are just putting in the minimum, then you will get back the minimum.

Actually, I believe that your results are actually one step below your input. Meaning that if you put in an average effort, you get poor results. If you put in good effort, you get average results. BUT, if you put in great effort, you get great results because most people do not put in great effort. So if you do that level of work, you get that level of rewards.

Again, you don't need to be as funny as any big-name comedian, but you can become funnier if you do the work. You can be a "1-percenter" in the ranks of business presenters. Remember, when you're funnier, people like you more, and that will increase the chances of their doing business with you.

The point is, if you want to be great, then you need to *do the work*! Am I sounding like a broken record? Good. Because I promise you that if you do the work of adding humor, it will pay off (and then give me all the credit, please!).

A great way to motivate you to do the work for your presentations is to ask yourself, 'what if this is the last presentation you will ever give?' How do you want to be remembered by your LAST audience?

The amazing (and crazy) Tracey Morgan once told me, 'Don't give them a show, give them an experience.' So give your audience an experience by using humor because I can promise you that most audiences are bored to tears during your competitors' presentations.

More inspiration to 'do the work' comes from a recent unsolicited quote I received the other day:

> Thanks for the great presentation you gave at GoBundance, I used your recommendations and absolutely crushed my sales presentation at the conference. Was told I was a stand out speaker and was really able to get the crowd engaged with some humor. You the man!
> —Ryan Hughes, 360 Risk Partners

Do you want to be a stand out speaker? Yes, yes you do… that is why you are reading this book!

WHEN TO USE HUMOR IN YOUR PRESENTATION

As I mentioned earlier, you have most certainly heard that you should start every presentation with a joke because it helps make an emotional connection with the audience right away.

I suggest that you do the work and write one-minute of jokes about yourself that you can use at the start of almost every presentation. Once this is done, you will have polished and perfected jokes that are almost guaranteed to work. And then if for some reason a joke falls flat, have a joke for that, too.

I tell my clients that if a joke I wrote for them doesn't get a laugh, say something like, "I paid a professional joke writer to write me that joke. And obviously I didn't pay him enough, or else you people would be laughing right now."

As discussed earlier, the other place you need to add your humor is at transition points and just before your key message.

I'm a firm believer in leading by example. And one of the things I do for business executives is enhance their presentations by adding color and humor. So let's move forward to do some real "presentation punch-ups."

Even if you fall on your face, you're still moving forward.

CHAPTER 10

PRESENTATION PUNCH-UP EXAMPLES

L et's do a punch-up together, shall we? I know this seems to be a one-sided conversation, so now you know how my wife feels.

One of my clients is an amazing person named Paul Akers who is a very successful inventor and a world leader in Lean management consulting.

Paul is modest enough and smart enough, however, to know that he doesn't know it all. And he appreciates the wisdom of adding humor to his presentations. Of course, I say that because he asked me to help punch up his presentations. Let me walk you through it using my three-step process.

When discussing efficiency, Paul asked the audience:

"How long will it take you to change a tire? Some of you would say thirty minutes; some of you would say an hour."

How could this be improved? First up, in the statements of truth, I thought about all the things that come to mind when changing a tire.

STATEMENTS OF TRUTH

Subject: Changing a tire
Changing a tire gets your hands dirty.
Changing a tire on the side of the road is dangerous.
Spare tire is usually in the trunk.
Some people don't know how to change a tire.
Some people call AAA to change their tire.
The spare tire is usually much smaller and called a donut.
Many flat tires are caused by nails in the road.

Now you fill in some of the blanks:

_____

_____

_____

_____

_____

Now we move on to the lists. What words can you think of when it comes to changing a tire? Here is what I came up with:

LISTS

Subject: Changing a tire

cars	AAA	side of the road
small tire	instructions	running late
donut tire	do it yourself	greasy hands
dangerous	lift	getting dirty
lug nuts	trunk	wrench
nails	potholes	glass

Now you fill in some of the blanks:

If you are paying attention, you will see that I like using as many words as possible that have hard consonants, just like I did with my earlier example for *traffic*.

I will pick the words with the hard consonants and finish the sentences in the next step.

Now we move onto the exercise of "I (emotion) (subject) because___," starting off with *hate*.

"I (emotion) (subject) because: _____"
I hate changing tires because:

> I want to wait on AAA.
> I think it's dangerous.
> I don't like getting dirty on my way to work.
> I don't want to empty my trunk to get my spare tire.
> I don't want to ride around on a small tire.
> I am scared the car will fall on me.

Now you fill in some of the blanks:

_____

_____

_____

_____

_____

We then replace the word *hate* with the word *love*, and we are now able to start to see some funny:

"I (emotion) (subject) because: _____"
I love changing tires because:

I like waiting on AAA.

I live for danger.

I like getting dirty on my way to work.

I get to be reminded of what all is in my trunk.

I like it when one tire is smaller than the others.

I like the thrill of having the car possibly fall on me.

Now you fill in some of the blanks:

I love changing tires because:

_____

_____

_____

_____

_____

Are they hilarious? No. Are they even funny? Not really. But they're a starting point. These sentences start to put perspective on the subject.

Let's look at the original question again:

"How long will it take you to change a tire? Some of you would say thirty minutes; some of you would say an hour."

So let's use the exercise of misdirection to see if we can find something funnier.

MISDIRECTION

Write the sentence:

> *"How long will it take you to change a tire? Some of you would say thirty minutes; some of you would say an hour."*

Verbs/nouns/adjectives/prepositions:
Change tire, how long, some, say, thirty minutes, an hour

Opposite and associated verbs, nouns, adjectives, prepositions, etc.:
AAA, going fast, no time, infinite time, many, most, none, ten minutes, forty minutes, twenty seconds, thirty seconds, twenty hours, thirty hours

Now you fill in some of the blanks:

——————— ——————— ———————
——————— ——————— ———————
——————— ——————— ———————

I am putting down the first thoughts that come to my mind. Remember, don't edit what is coming out of you; edit once it is already out of you.

Now we start to mix up these opposite words with the sentence to see what funny angle we can take on the sentence.

MISDIRECTION

"How long will it take you to change a tire? Some of you would say thirty minutes; some of you would say an hour."

Some people say twenty to thirty hours.
It will take ten minutes to change the tire.
I will wait on AAA to change the tire.
It will take as long as it takes for AAA to arrive.
It will take about ten minutes after AAA arrives.

Now you fill in some of the blanks:

_____

_____

_____

_____

_____

You could, therefore, answer the question with this nugget:

"How long will it take you to change a tire? Some of you would say thirty minutes; some of you would say an hour. And some of you would say about ten minutes after AAA arrives."

Again, this is not meant to be LOL. It is meant to be "he-he." It's just a nice little bit of humor to keep the audience engaged.

Another point Paul discussed in his presentation was how he sometimes e-mails his ideas to seventy people to get immediate feedback. He explains:

I e-mail it to seventy beta testers and they reply with:

1) *Gotta have it right now.*
2) *Good idea.*
3) *Don't waste your time.*

Now, since these responses are enumerated, we can add one to the list to let that be the "surprise ending." If you do the "three-step process," the main subject was sending an e-mail to seventy people. Use the subject of "e-mailing" and almost certainly the word "spam" is on your list.

When I think of "spam," I think of "take me off your list." So, if you do the exercises, you could come up with this gem:

I e-mail it to seventy beta testers and they reply with:

1) *Gotta have it right now.*
2) *Good idea.*
3) *Don't waste your time*
   and...
4) *Please take me off your list.*

Paul used these jokes, and others, with success. Of course, we also rehearsed when he should pause for dramatic effect, as well as what words to emphasize and how to emphasize them. In the end, the humor added to the presentation, but it required Paul's willingness to invest his time to make it happen.

Another benefit of learning how to find the "funny" in your presentations will help you find the "funny" in your life. Paul said his wife of thirty-three years is now finding him funny thanks to the work we did together. And since making someone laugh means they like you more, that means she likes him more and that means I am also a marriage counselor.

CHAPTER 11

Punching Up Steve Jobs

The power of humor was fully appreciated and used by one of the most successful business-men of our generation who was also one of the best presenters. His name: Steve Jobs.

But even a great presenter can improve! So I've audaciously punched up one of Steve Jobs's most famous speeches: his 2005 commencement address to Stanford University. I focus on key phrases he used at the beginning and at transition points.

Watch his presentations (you can find them on YouTube), and you'll see that he elicits quite a few chuckles.

I understand that Jobs was known for spending at least eight hours getting ready for a presentation. How much hourly income do you think Steve Jobs earned? Just think: he spent eight times that amount preparing to go on stage. How much do *you* invest preparing for your speeches, presentations, and/or parole hearings?

If putting the preparation time into a presentation is good enough for Steve Jobs, it should be good enough for you!

So here goes. Here are his quotes:

Thank you! I am honored to speak to you today for your commencement from one of the finest universities in the world. Truth be told, I never graduated from college, and this is the closest I ever got into a college graduation.

Let's just look at that word *college.* What do you picture when you think about college? What do you visualize when you think about a college graduation ceremony?

This time, I want you to do this exercise on your own. Don't be scared. *Do not* look ahead until you have done the exercises. I have done this exercise, too, but let's see how well you do first.

You can do these exercises in the writing exercises provided in the back of this book, or in a Word document on your computer.

I have also provided all these exercises for free by going to www.HumorWins.com/resources.

OK. I hope you did the work. If you did, you can proceed to read my answers! If you didn't—go do the work!

Here is my version:

STATEMENTS OF TRUTH

Subject: College

College is fun.

College is expensive, and you get in debt with college loans.

College creates lifetime friends.

College degrees earn you more money.

College makes you more well-rounded.

College graduation marks a new chapter in people's lives.

Most people do not work in the field of their college degree.

Some people go to the military to pay for their college.

Now we move on to the next step of listing words associated with college.

LISTS

Subject: College

tuition	scholarships	student debt
student loans	late nights	partying
dating	studying	sports

graduation   Greek system   professors

cap and gown   part-time jobs   concerts

GI Bill   Ramen noodles   pizza

long-term debt   late night studying

college sweethearts college roommates

"I (emotion) (subject) because: _____ "
I hate college because:

I don't like being poor.
I don't like spending the rest of my life paying back student loans.
I don't like how I look in a gap and gown.
I don't like living on Ramen noodles.
I don't like to study.
I don't like being in debt.
Roommates are usually messy and loud.

"I (emotion) (subject) because: _____ "
I love college because:

Being poor is so much fun.
I look forward to paying off college loans for the rest of my life.
I look good in a cap and gown.
I find Ramen noodles delicious.
Studying is so much fun.
Being in debt builds character.

I get to live with people who test my patience.

So, how funny would it be if Steve Jobs had said…

*"Truth be told. This is the closest I have ever got into a college graduation, **and believe it or not, I am still paying off my student loans.**"*

or

*"Truth be told. This is the closest I have ever got into a college graduation, **and I like wearing this cap and gown. It helps cover up my recent weight gain.**"*

See how humor enhances those phrases?

In this exercise, we took *college* and dissected it in order to expand it. This expansion allowed us to find words and references to connect some dots to find what tickles the funny bone. If you can write humor by just "going by your gut"—that's great. But, most of the time if you try that, you will get brain freeze. So until you have built that comedy muscle, use the structure of the three-step process to formulate some real humor.

OK, now let's look at a transition point. Here is a key quote from a transition point in Mr. Jobs's speech:

Woz and I started Apple in my parents' garage when I was twenty. We worked hard, and in ten years Apple had grown from just the two of us in a garage into a $2 billion company with over four *thousand employees. We had just released our finest creation—the Macintosh—a year earlier, and I had just turned thirty. And then I got fired. How can you get fired from a company you started?*

Of all these phrases, I think the one that we should focus on is the last line and ask, "*How can you get fired from a company you started?*"

Let's look at that sentence, and do the exercises again. Please don't take a sneak peek ahead to see my version. Do your own first.

STATEMENTS OF TRUTH

Subject: Being fired

Being fired is embarrassing.

When you get fired, you sometimes get a severance package.

Some people collect unemployment after being fired.

People usually get fired for being lazy or insubordinate, for bad behavior, or for embarrassing oneself at the company Christmas party.

Nobody likes being fired.

You have to carry out a box of your things when you are fired.

You have to turn in company-owned property when you are fired.

LISTS

Subject: Being fired

lost job	Christmas party	espionage
laid off	company picnic	disrespectful
severance	being late package	showing up drunk
embezzlement	sexual harassment	being lazy
lying	being rude	insubordination
bad decisions	not being a team player	broke

Now pick your favorite words from the list above and finish the sentence in the next step:

"I (emotion) (subject) because: _____ "
I hate being fired because:

I don't like telling people I lost my job.
I don't like collecting unemployment.
I don't like being broke.

I need my benefits.
I like being productive.
But I love insubordination.
(Note the variance of replacing *because* with *but* because that can lead to other surprise endings.)
But that was the best Christmas party ever.
But that was the best company picnic ever.

And then switch from hate to love to get:

"I (emotion) (subject) because: _____"
I love being fired because:

I like telling people I lost my job.
I like collecting unemployment.
Being broke is a great way to go through life.
Now I get to pay triple for my benefits.
Now I have no excuse to be productive.
Being insubordinate always has its own rewards.
I find Christmas parties to be one of my key weaknesses.
I hate company picnics.

In my opinion, it would be funny if Steve Jobs had said,

"How can you get fired from a company you started? Does this mean I have to pay myself unemployment?"

Do you see how the exercise works? We are taking this one sentence; we are coming at it from different angles; we are looking at the adjectives, verbs, and nouns; we are dissecting and expanding it; we are reversing it; and then using the feeling from our "gut." That's how you "find the funny."

Now consider the final transition point of Mr. Jobs's awesome speech:

> *My third story is about death. When I was seventeen, I read a quote that went something like: "If you live each day as if it was your last, some day you'll most certainly be right."*

OK, admittedly this is a difficult one to punch up so I will save you the trouble of doing the three-step process and let you know that you can find the "funny" in this sentence by using the misdirection exercise. (What a relief!)

Again, there are blank pages in the back of this book to use, or make a Word document, or download all the exercises by going to www.HumorWins. com/resources.

And if you are thinking, "I will just do that later," then you can keep reading.

MISDIRECTION

Write the sentence:
If you live each day as if it was your last, some day you'll most certainly be right.

Verbs/nouns/adjectives/prepositions:
Live, each, day, your last, last, some, certainly, right

Opposite and associated verbs, nouns, adjectives, prepositions, etc.:
Die, get by, every, always, all, mine, ours, first, all, many, guessing, wrong

MISDIRECTION

"If you live each day as if it was your last, some day you'll most certainly be right.."

If you live each night as it were your last, you will probably die.

If you live each day as if it's just another day, you will always be unsure.

If you live each day like it is your first, you will always be wrong.

Now, I think it would have been somewhat humorous if after saying, "*If you live each day as if it was your last, some day you'll most certainly be right,*" Mr. Jobs had added:

> "*And if you live each day as if it were your first, you will always be wrong.*"

CHAPTER 12

PUNCHING UP "THE HIDDEN LEADER" SPEECH

Here's another example from a speech I punched up for a client of mine named Scott Edinger.

Scott's presentation about leadership was called "The Hidden Leader," and at one point, he uses the analogy of a football quarterback.

He wrote:

In order to throw the football, the QB stands with shoulders facing down field. When that happens they turn their backs to defenders who are running to smash into them. That creates a vulnerable "blind side" that the line must protect.

I added:

In the military, it is called "I got your six," which means I have your back, as in six o'clock. So the line protects the QB's six, so he can score six points and another $6 million bonus.

This works because most people know that quarterbacks are extravagantly well paid so, if nothing else, it raises a smile.

Scott went on to discuss the extraordinary amount of work done by people at various levels within a company that is often not obvious—what he calls "the hidden leaders."

He wrote:

I've been so impressed by these professionals, the offensive line of an organization, that I wanted to write about them and help you recognize them in your own organization.

I added a line:

I've been so impressed by these professionals, the offensive line of an organization, that I wanted to write about them and help you recognize them in your own organization. *And these hidden leaders are not as easy to spot as an offensive lineman.*

Again, let me be the first to acknowledge that this is not hilarious stuff. But it is striking the right kind of tone.

Later in his speech, Scott talked about hidden leaders having integrity and gave the example of a company with which he'd worked that was launching a new product. He knew that quite a few of the attendees at a meeting to discuss the launch schedule had serious reservations, but were concerned that the CEO and president wouldn't take criticism well. So they feigned praise or said nothing. Until one woman (let's call her Mary) bravely spoke up, sharing a dissenting and well-thought-out point of view.

HIS VERSION

As expected, the executives didn't like the feedback and argued hotly that she had a myopic perspective, was being too negative, and that they had the experience to make it work.

The whole room went silent for several minutes. She maintained her position and cited clear examples of client situations that supported her feedback. Mary's integrity in taking an unpopular position for the sake of the customers and the company began to galvanize the others in the room.

Finally, though it took a while, other employees began to defend Mary's points and share their own criticisms.

Ultimately, faced with the overwhelming and anecdotal evidence that the program was not yet ready for prime time, the CEO and president listened.

MY VERSION
I punched it up with the inserts italicized and in bold below.

As expected, the executives didn't like the feedback and argued hotly that she had a myopic perspective, was being too negative, and that they had the experience to make it work.

The whole room went silent for several minutes. ***By the time Mary responded, it felt like I could have read* War and Peace.**

She maintained her position and cited clear examples of client situations that supported her feedback. Mary's integrity in taking an unpopular position for the sake of the customers and the company began to galvanize the others in the room.

Finally, though it took a while, other employees began to defend Mary's points and share their own criticisms.

...mostly of Mary, but still...

Hopefully they did that while* not *updating their resumes.

Scott says he notices that using the humor we came up with together has made a dramatic difference in his audience engagement.

So that's how you can punch up presentations with words. There's another way that's even easier—and that's by using visual aids.

CHAPTER 13

SELF-DEPRECATING HUMOR

As I mentioned earlier, Johnny Carson said that if you are likable, you have 80 percent of the battle won. When I first started in stand-up comedy, I was not likable on stage. I thought I was smarter than the audience and came across as a dick. About 1/3 of the audience loved me, while 2/3 hated me. After a while I realized that my childhood dream was to make people laugh, not piss them off.

So in order to be a better person, I worked on myself offstage. I figured if I am going to get on stage and be myself with the audience, then I need to be the best person I can be.

And through this self-discovery, I came up with a formula for likability:

CONFIDENCE + HUMILITY = LIKABILITY
People who are confident but not humble are typically not likable.

People who are humble but not confident are typically not likable.

When you mix the two together, that is when you are likable. And one of the best ways for business leaders to show humility is through the use of self-deprecating jokes.

Self-deprecation, making fun of yourself, is probably the safest form of humor. Hey, look who you're "offending." It's you! What are *you* going to do about it?

> Self-deprecating humor makes leaders appear more likable, trusting, and caring.
> —*INC.* magazine, August, 2014

> Self-deprecation is disarming and makes others feel included.
> —*Forbes*, August, 2012

A couple of rules for self-deprecating humor:

a) Don't go too harshly on yourself as you don't want to make people feel uncomfortable
b) Don't lie about yourself. Nobody wants to hear an attractive person talking about how hideous they are. (I found that out firsthand.) Stay authentic.

A master of the art (an old master if you like) was President Ronald Reagan who deftly turned concerns about his age to his advantage.

Here are just a couple of quotes from his speeches:

> "Jefferson once said…We should never judge a president by his age but only by his work… (pause)…and ever since he told me that…"

Boom! Lots of laughter. It was a brilliant line delivered with perfection, which is what you'd expect from such a seasoned actor.

In the same vein, Reagan also added: "Just to show you how youthful I am I intend to campaign in all thirteen states."

Big laughs!

Reagan wasn't the only president to use self-deprecating humor. Abraham Lincoln used it to great effect many years earlier. Lincoln was not regarded as a handsome man, a fact on which he capitalized in one of his first debates when his opponent accused him of being "two-faced." (I guess it was still a secret back then that politicians are liars. But regardless, Lincoln was one of the best presenters in US history for the past four score and whatever years ago.)

Anyway, after his opponent kept calling him "two-faced," Honest Abe's clever retort was, "Sir, if I had two faces would I be wearing this one?"

There are two types of self-deprecating jokes:

a) Obvious: making fun of your own characteristics that are visible (as Lincoln did.)
b) Nonobvious: making fun of your characteristics that are not visible.

My obvious:

"I have so much gray hair that I look like Anderson Cooper's older brother."

My nonobvious:

"My apathy causes me problems, but I don't really care."

Everyone can learn to do self-deprecation if you just follow this formula. Yes, we have a methodology for that, too.

THE SELF-DEPRECATION METHODOLOGY

Step One:
Write down both your obvious and non-obvious characteristics and then pick one of these traits.

Now follow the steps we have done previously in the Three-Step Process.

Step Two: Write your "statements of truth" on that unique trait.

Step Three: List adjectives, nouns, etc., connected with that trait.

Step Four: I (emotion) (trait) because...

Personal Example

So let me, once again, practice what I preach, step up to the plate, and go first.

MARSHALL CHILES: UNIQUE CHARACTERISTICS OBVIOUS/PHYSICAL

I have gray hair.
I am average height.
I look like Flea from the Red Hot Chili Peppers.

NON-OBVIOUS/NON-PHYSICAL
I grew up poor.
I am married with two kids.
I am scared about ending up at the wrong end of the food chain.

I am going to write about the obvious characteristic of "gray hair."

STATEMENTS OF TRUTH

Subject: Gray hair

Gray hair makes you look older.
Gray hair makes you look distinguished.
Anderson Cooper is known for having all gray hair.
Steve Martin is known for having all gray hair.
Some people color their gray hair.
Some people get gray hair from stress.
Some people are attracted to gray hair.

LISTS

Subject: Gray hair

old	distinguished	aged
stressed	attractive	investor
grandfather	ashy	executive
gray fox	salt and pepper	retired
Anderson Cooper	Steve Martin	shaved
hair dye	Just For Men	coloring

slow driver   The Villages   Florida

"I (emotion) (subject) because: _____"
I hate having gray hair because:

The word distinguished is just a nice way for saying I look old.
I don't like being called grandpa.
It does not look attractive on my back.
Now I have to pay attention to "Just For Men" commercials.
People say I look like Anderson Cooper.
People keep asking me when I am moving to The Villages.
But I love the senior discounts.
(Note the variance of replacing *because* with *but* because that can lead to another surprise ending.)
But at least now I look distinguished.

"I (emotion) (subject) because: _____"
I love having gray hair because:

Looking distinguished makes people think I am rich.
I like getting the respect of a grandfather.
Some girls find it attractive.
Now I pay attention to commercials for "Just For Men."
Anderson Cooper and Steve Martin have made it fashionable.
I get the early bird specials in Florida.

The jokes I use for this trait when I am on stage are:

> "I know what most of you are thinking... so that's what Flea from the Red Hot Chili Peppers looks like with gray hair."

> "I have so much gray hair that people think I am Anderson Cooper's older brother."

Note that I used a character trait of looking like Flea and combined it with the gray hair trait. The original Flea joke I wrote was "...so that's what Flea from the Red Hot Chili Peppers looks like with his shirt on." I then changed it to *gray hair* in order to bridge to the Anderson Cooper joke. The Flea–gray hair joke is actually a bread crumb to lead to the next joke.

An additional joke to referencing that I look like Anderson Cooper is: "I'm what Anderson Cooper would look like if CNN didn't have a nutritionist on staff." Now I am making fun of not being as "fit" as Anderson Cooper.

Now it's *your* turn. Do these exercises now while the information is fresh in your head. Take the next ten to fifteen minutes to complete the following exercises to find self-deprecating jokes:

Your Unique Characteristics
Obvious

_____

_____

_____

_____

_____

_____

Nonobvious:

_____

_____

_____

_____

_____

_____

Pick one of those characteristics from either the obvious or nonobvious:

Statements of Truth

Characteristic: _____

_____
_____
_____
_____
_____
_____
_____

Lists

Characteristic: _____

_____ _____ _____
_____ _____ _____
_____ _____ _____
_____ _____ _____
_____ _____ _____
_____ _____ _____
_____ _____ _____
_____ _____ _____
_____ _____ _____
_____ _____ _____
_____ _____ _____
_____ _____ _____

"I (emotion) (characteristic) because: _____"
   I hate _____ because:

_____

_____

_____

_____

_____

_____

_____

"I (emotion) (characteristic) because: _____"
   I love _____ because:

_____

_____

_____

_____

_____

_____

_____

Write Some Funny Lines about Your Unique Characteristic:

_____

_____

_____

_____

_____

_____

_____

Let me tell you that in the real world of business, self-deprecation can definitely be a winner.

I once worked with the CEO of a four-hundred-person company. He had recently bought the business for $500 million and then fired the founder and the entire C-suite. That's not a move that's likely to make you popular with those four hundred employees.

Four months later at the holiday party, the CEO had to stand up in front of a room crowded with unhappy and worried employees. How could he win them over?

He hired Humor Wins to write a fifteen-minute, self-deprecating routine for him and all the new C-suite team members he'd brought into the company. It defused the situation, humanized him, and made his employees laugh. They felt like they knew him better and that he was likable, in spite of everything that had gone before.

Knowing the power of humor, and especially self-deprecating humor, is why my client hired me to write his holiday party speech. Here are some sample jokes where the names have been changed to protect the innocent:

> *"Tommy our Production Director use to work for Acme, then left to come to Globex. And now Acme has <u>bought</u> Globex, so Tommy wakes up everyday*

working back at Acme. Tommy is like Bill Murray in Groundhog Day. Except Bill Murray can actually deliver.

OK, now let's talk about Finance. The most interesting thing we can say about finance is how handsome and well dressed our CFO John Robinson is.
John is known for having great hair, being fashionable, and is paid lots of money for being himself... he is like the Kim Kardashian of Acme.
John once said that if he could have just one superpower, it would be to never get sick. It's probably because he doesn't want the fever to mess up his hair.

And for those that don't know, our COO Karen is a <u>great</u> hockey player. Because nothing says sensitive leader, like a body check.
When designing our new offices, it took us weeks to talk her out of putting in a penalty box.
Apparently I am still in trouble for high sticking (?), and I don't even know what that means. It sounds like an HR problem to me.
Karen hasn't missed a day of work in 14 years, but she <u>is</u> missing 8 teeth. "

The result was that everybody laughed while getting to know him and the new leadership team. Plus people felt more comfortable around him in the office. This new sense of camaraderie helped make these big changes more palatable for the 400 employees.

With a $500 million investment, it was well worth paying me to write that speech. In hindsight, I should have charged more!

So again, I suggest you do the work, or pay someone to do it (hint-hint) in order to make a greater impact on your audience.

Content is critical. But even great content is a waste of time if you don't also learn how to deliver the lines. More on that subject in the next chapter.

CHAPTER 14

DELIVERY

E ven if you have the best jokes in the world, if you cannot deliver them well, they will not be as effective.

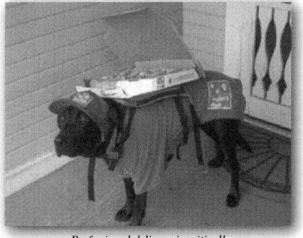

Professional delivery is critical!

Some notes on delivery:

1) Know which words to emphasize.
   The key bread crumbs and the punch word(s) need to be accentuated to better help lead your audience.

2) Pauses
   When you pause in the right place, it allows your audience to go down the projected road. Pauses enhances misdirection.

It is very important to pause after your punch word/line in order to let the audience process and laugh.

A very important key is to not "step on your laughs." That means to let the audience laugh before starting your next sentence. A very common mistake by newbie comedians is that they are so excited they got a laugh that they can't wait to get onto the next joke.

Jeff Garlin told me: "Let your jokes sizzle." That means to let the laughter sizzle, and then move on when it is not sizzling.

Remember the Mitch Hedberg joke from earlier?

> "This shirt is dry clean only. Which
> means (pause) it's dirty."

The pause just after *which means* lets the audience go down their own projected path.

3) Go twice as slow.
   Comedian Buddy Hackett **says to go twice as slowly** as you think you are going because, chances are, you are actually going twice as fast as you think you are going.

   He also said that when you go slowly enough, it doubles your laughs per minute because during your pauses, the audience will "write" their own jokes and laugh at those. Then when they hear your punch line, they laugh at that—doubling your laughs per joke.

But nothing is better for your delivery than:

4) Rehearse. Rehearse. Rehearse.
   As we all know, if you want to be good at anything, you need to practice. And as Malcolm Gladwell pointed out in his awesome book *Outliers*, if you want to be great at it, you really need to do it 10,000 times.

   Many people flat out refuse to rehearse. They might spend some time putting their text and graphics together, but then when it comes time to practice their presentation, they can't be bothered to put in the hours.

   Remember, Steve Jobs would spend eight hours rehearsing for a presentation. You can be sure Ronald Reagan wasn't averse to rehearsals, either. Take a play from their play books, and do the work.

Using a Bail Line

If a joke falls flat, there's an easy way out that will almost certainly get the laugh you were looking for. Blame the humor guy.

As I mentioned earlier, you can say something like:

"Oh, well. I hired a humor guy to add humor here. I guess I didn't pay him enough."

"I took lessons from a humor guy. I guess I should have paid for another session."

"Man, that sounded a lot funnier in the car on the way here."

"I guess I have nothing but yes-men around me because my staff told me that was a funny joke."

Writing a few saver jokes to keep in your pocket is a great idea. And if you don't have a saver joke, at least use some of the ones I've shared with you so if the joke doesn't work, you have a way of relating to their not laughing at it.

CHAPTER 15

The Big Closer

Congratulations, you've made it to the last chapter. You're on your way to Comedy Central (or whatever the corporate world equivalent is... the Berkshire Hathaway executive retreat?)

So, let's recap. Humor is important because, when you present, you are trying to persuade people to take action or change their beliefs.

Remember Dr. Jim Lyttle's work..."Humor increases persuasion's effectiveness." That was back in the olden days of 1977. And guess what... it still works.

Group Communication

Forbes magazine published a study showing that effective humor increases the quantity and quality of group communications. The key word is *effective.* Ineffective humor, on the other hand, makes people want to leave the room. So follow the humor rules and guidelines in this book, and you will be fine.

Let's review the "methodologies of mirth." (I just wrote that because I like the alliteration.)

PRESENTATION PUNCH-UP
In a presentation punch-up, all you do is:

1) Write your presentation without trying to be humorous.
2) Take the first sentence where you want to add the funny and put it on a separate sheet of paper.
3) Write as much humor about that sentence as possible.
4) Put it back in the presentation.
5) Do it again.

Step three in the above process can be written using this methodology:

THREE-STEP PROCESS
Step One: Write your statements of truth.
Step Two: Write your lists: same, opposite, hard consonants, and emotional words.
Step Three: I (emotion) (subject) because___

And you can also use this exercise:

MISDIRECTION

Make people think you are taking them one way, but then change course. Make sure the new path matches the beginning of both the projected and surprise path.

ADDING FUNNY IMAGES

1) Go to Google Images and enter the words *funny* plus the "subject" of your key message.
2) Find an image that can apply to the subject.
3) Write the sentence that matches the subject and the funny image.

QUANTITY = QUALITY

The more you do, the better you will be at it. (It is a universal truth.)

Don't edit what is coming out of you; edit once it is already out of you.

And last but not least…

THE HUMOR RULES

Humor is safe comedy.

1) Keep it above the belt.
2) Stay away from religion and politics.

3) Do not make fun of any one person or group of people.
4) Stay away from words with violent images.
5) Stay away from references to drugs.
Stay away from unsafe subjects.

Do you see a rule missing? There is one rule that is not here on purpose. Can you figure out what it is?

The biggest rule of all, which does not need to be written—but is always understood—is: "no cursing." Especially when used in external communications because you never know who might be offended.

I have a seven-year-old son who has been really... pushing his boundaries, shall we say. He just got in trouble at school for cursing when he said to another classmate: "You are f-ing crazy." Now granted, I am glad he used it in a grammatically correct way, but still, he is a seven-year-old saying the f-word at school.

His teacher was standing right behind him and she responded, "*Nolan!* What did you say?"

My son turned around, looked up at her in surprise and said, "I didn't know you were there."

Nolan's mistake is a prime example of why when you want to be funny, you need to consider the setting. In a work setting, you need to follow the rules outlined earlier, because you never know who is going to be listening!

So you've discovered there is a serious side to being funny. It's work—just like any other job. But when you nail it, you'll get unbelievable results.

You'll go beyond being the entertaining speaker to being the speaker who gets results because your audience actually listens to you, takes critical information onboard, and puts it into action. The results are increased engagement and likability, which lead to sales and increased profits.

As Steve Martin put it so well,

"Be so good they can't ignore you."
Go break a leg.

ABOUT THE AUTHOR

I knew at the age of seven I wanted to be a comedian. I learned early on that if you can make people laugh, they will accept you and probably not beat you up at the bus stop.

My comedy experience has been fantastic, and I wouldn't trade it for anything in the world. I have never understood why so much of corporate America is against being funny at work. Hence, why I figured out "The Humor Rules."

This book is my first official "brain dump" as to why and how I see comedy helping make this world a better place, by showing those working in the business world how to use humor in their presentations. My hope is that seeing the many benefits of humor will help bring more humor to the work place… and more people to comedy clubs!

If you liked this book, do me a huge favor and go see an 'unknown' comedian at a local comedy club this week.

Appendix A

Exercises

These exercises can also be found at www. HumorWins.com/resources

The Three-Step Process

Statements of Truth

Characteristic: _____

_____

_____

_____

_____

_____

_____

_____

_____

_____

_____

_____

_____

_____

_____

LISTS

Characteristic: _____

"I (emotion) (characteristic) because: _____"
    I hate _____ because:

_____

_____

_____

_____

_____

_____

_____

_____

_____

_____

_____

_____

_____

_____

_____

_____

_____

_____

_____

_____

"I (emotion) (characteristic) because: _____"
    I love _____ because:

_____
_____
_____
_____
_____
_____
_____
_____
_____
_____
_____
_____
_____
_____
_____
_____
_____
_____
_____

Write Some Funny Lines about Your Unique Characteristic:

_____

_____

_____

_____

_____

_____

_____

_____

_____

_____

_____

_____

_____

_____

Self-Deprecating Jokes

Your Unique Characteristics

Obvious:

_____
_____
_____
_____
_____
_____

Nonobvious:

_____
_____
_____
_____
_____
_____

Pick one of those characteristics from either the obvious or nonobvious:

STATEMENTS OF TRUTH

Characteristic: _____

_____

_____

_____

_____

_____

_____

LISTS

Characteristic: _____

"I (emotion) (characteristic) because: _____"
    I hate _____ because:

_____

_____

_____

_____

_____

_____

_____

_____

_____

_____

_____

_____

"I (emotion) (characteristic) because: _____"
    I love _____ because:

_____

_____

_____

_____

_____

_____

_____

_____

_____

_____

_____

_____

Write Some Funny Lines about Your Unique Characteristic:

_____

_____

_____

APPENDIX B

JOKE WRITING SERVICES

My goal is to make this world a better place through comedy. I love the sound of laughter and think that if we had more laughter in our world, especially in corporate America, this world would be a better place.

Yes, I have shown you how to find and create the funny yourself. And if you follow the methodology I have shared, then you can do it yourself.

Regardless, many people have hired me to write the funny for them, which is fine too. So we at Humor Wins have come up with a few services:

1. **Custom Clean Jokes**: We add the funny to your presentations, newsletters, custody battles, etc. You give us the material you want to add humor to and then we do our magic and give it back to you.
2. **Executive Humor Coaching**: We help you be funnier on your own by working hand-in-hand going over our methodologies with you. The end goal is that you will be able to find the funny on your own much quicker than before we worked with you.

   And if you want to have some real fun...
3. **Corporate Comedy Roasts**: We provide a custom comedy show base don the people in the room. This unique, fun experience has been quoted as 'one of the best events in company history' per several clients.

We hope our services are able to help you make your world a better place by bringing more laughter to your organization, clients and prospects. To learn more, please visit: www.HumorWins.com

Made in the USA
San Bernardino, CA
22 June 2016